THE ILLUSTRATOR'S LIBRARY

Pencil

C O N T E N T S

Introduction

Have you noticed that some people tell a story very well? They seem to have a gift for choosing words. They know how to use language to capture and hold the attention of their listeners. Some people can do the same thing with pictures, and this form of storytelling is called illustration.

Storytelling is both ancient and honored. Most of the evidence of the past has come to us through words, songs, and pictures. The artists among the cave dwellers have left us a record of actual hunting scenes. The designers of ancient languages created pictures with symbols from everyday life. And a thousand years ago, when most people could not read, artists used the glorious colors of stained glass to tell stories from the Bible.

Today these examples of storytelling through pictures are considered great art. But in their own time these pictures were appreciated because they also provided information and entertainment. And today, with our advanced communications, the ability to tell a story well though illustration is more important than ever. The Illustrator's Library is designed to help you be the best storyteller you can be.

A preliminary sketch for the front cover. Visualizing paper.

C H A P T E R 1

Materials

Pencils, pencils, pencils—what would we do without pencils? A pencil is probably the most widely used writing tool in the world. Can you even imagine a world without pencils?

As common as it is, the pencil is a latecomer compared to other writing and drawing tools such as ink, pen, paint, and brush. What we call a "lead pencil" is really made from pure graphite, discovered in England in 1504. The graphite pencil took its place as a drawing tool alongside charcoal and silverpoint. Silverpoint, a shaped stick of silver, had for many years been a favorite drawing tool among artists but it was quickly replaced by the pencil.

Most artists then and now have used pencils for every kind of drawing from a rough sketch to a detailed finish. Famous artists such as Ingres, Delacroix, and Degas produced masterpieces of fine drawing with the pencil. Its versatility is probably the chief reason for its popularity; it can be used to produce almost any effect.

A pencil is also a great "idea catcher." Many illustrators keep pencil sketchbooks to record interesting sights or flights of fancy. Sometimes artists keep sketchbooks just for imaginative doodling. The next few pages will give you a closer look at the pencil in all its amazing variety.

A selection of tonal and textual effects; all done on strathmore kid finish paper (light texture). Pencils are listed above the rectangles.

Everyone is familiar with the common wooden or "bonded" pencil. Most artists' quality pencils come in that form. There is also a wooden carpenter's or sketch pencil; its graphite center is rectangular and can easily be sharpened into a chisel edge. Recently, the woodless pencil has become popular. This round, solid stick of graphite provides both a sharp point for detail and a broad edge for tone.

Mechanical pencils come in two basic styles. The ordinary type uses a very thin lead and needs no sharpening. The other type, preferred for drafting, uses thicker graphite sticks. They come in all degrees of hardness. These pencils usually require a special type of sharpener, although they also can be sharpened on a sandpaper block.

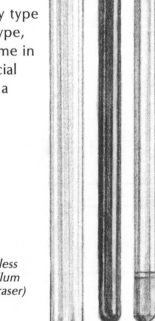

Right: sketching (carpenter's) pencil; center: woodless pencil; right: bonded, 6 sided, wooden pencil. (vellum tracing paper, 2H-5B pencils, ruler and kneaded eraser)

rubbed graphite dust   *4H-2H*   *4B woodless and ordinary eraser*   *4B pencil and water*

Sharpening and shaping your pencil requires a few basic tools and materials. The basic manual pencil sharpener may be used, but many illustrators prefer an electric sharpener because it is quicker and less likely to break the point as it sharpens. For sketching away from home (at museums, outdoors, and so on), take along a small pocket sharpener or a single-edged razor blade and a sandpaper block. (Remember to take a paper or plastic bag to catch all the sharpenings.)

You'll also need erasers—kneaded, gum, and plastic. The kneaded eraser is a very good all-around tool; use it not only for getting rid of mistakes but also for creating light tones and highlights.

Pocket and electric sharpeners; sandpaper block, vellum tracing paper, 2H-2B pencils

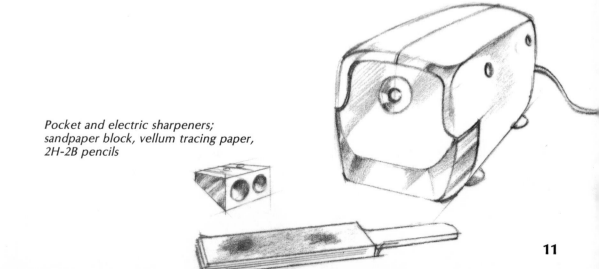

Left: top paper: pastel; bottom paper: Ledger bond, 3B pencil
Right: top paper: vellum tracing; bottom paper: ordinary newsprint, 2B-5B pencil

You ought to learn as much about paper as you can. Make an effort to get to an art store and ask to see a selection of drawing papers. These illustrations demonstrate how different papers can change the appearance of a drawing. Sometimes an artist will try one pencil after another to capture a certain quality without realizing that the solution is the paper, not the pencil. It is often

Top paper: strathmore kid finish (cold pressed)
Bottom paper: strathmore plate finish (hot
pressed), 3B pencil

too easy to keep drawing on the same type of pad, either because it is available or inexpensive. That would be a mistake.

Place two different kinds of paper side by side and draw on
them with a variety of pencils. Also, see how each paper reacts
to an eraser; that can be very important. Some papers take a
pencil beautifully, but tear and shred when erased.

A lightbox is one of the illustrator's most important pieces of equipment. It enables an artist to maintain a fresh and spontaneous quality in drawing. A simple lightbox can be made by putting an ordinary light bulb under a framed piece of glass or plastic.

You will need masking tape, a straight-edge ruler or T square, and a triangle or two. Some sort of fixative will be necessary to prevent smudging. (Remember to read the labels and observe all precautions when using spray cans.)

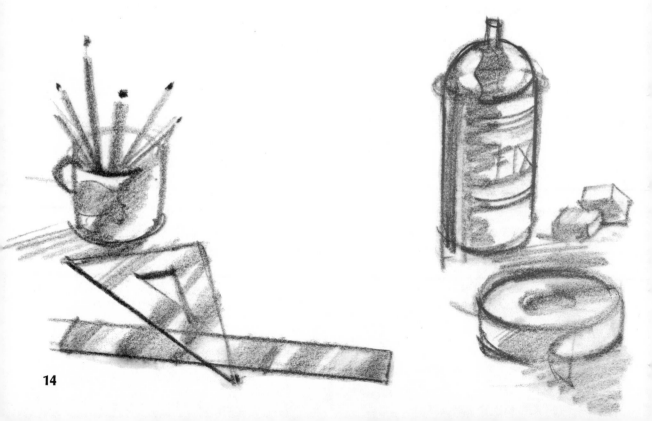

You will also need a desk or drawing board. Ideally, you should have a surface which is flat (not warped), square (to accommodate a T square) and adjustable in both height and angle. Your desk should be set up near a table with drawers or shelves to hold your materials.

All you need now is a good chair and you're ready to begin experimenting with pencils and paper.

All drawings done from real objects—very quickly using a 4B woodless pencil on ordinary tracing paper.

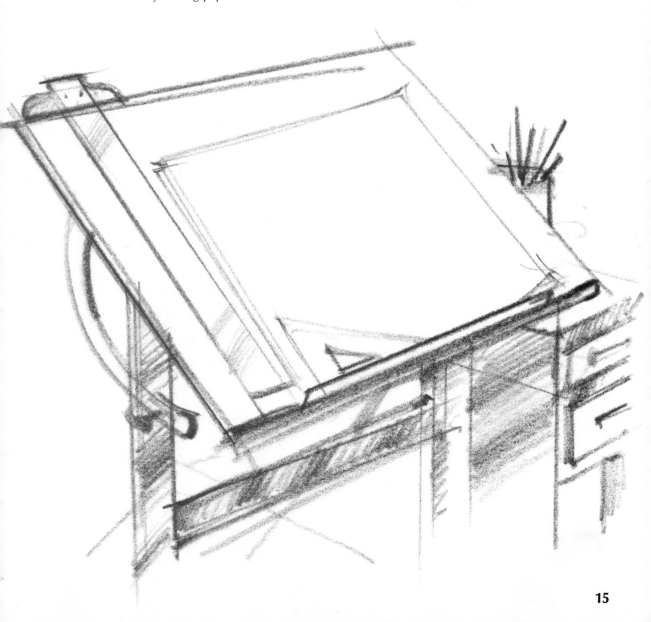

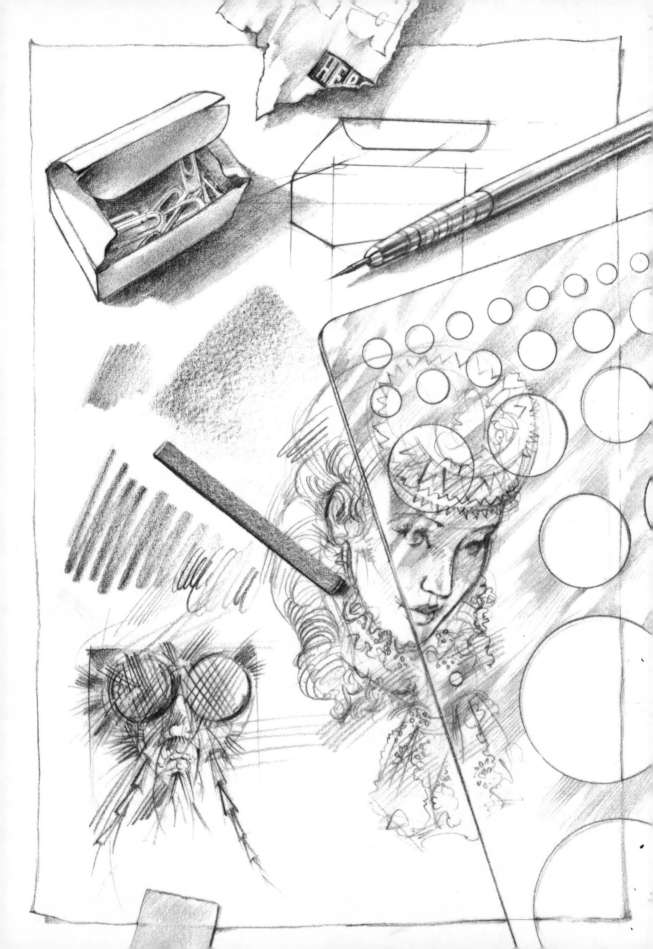

C H A P T E R 2

Techniques

There are probably as many ways of drawing with a pencil as there are artists. A drawing technique can become so personal and distinctive that an artist need not sign the picture for experts to know who made it. Usually this personal "touch" takes many years to develop. It is the result of experience and experiment. Since pencils come in many forms, various effects are possible, so you will have many opportunities to experiment with different approaches. Naturally, some ways of working will appeal to you more than others. The more you experiment the more likely you'll be to find your own special form of expression.

The illustration at the left shows some of the approaches you might consider and the materials you would use.

This type of illustration is called *trompe l'oeil*, a French term meaning "fool the eye." It is fun to do.

Begin simply. Place a box of paper clips or a candy wrapper on a piece of paper with some scribbles. Adjust your desk light to get a good shadow. Now try to draw the scene so that the box looks like it is really sitting on the paper. Pencil is the easiest medium to do this with because you can achieve all the necessary careful shading.

HB-5B—graphite stick—mechanical pencil with 2B lead; circle template; kneaded eraser for highlights; vellum tracing paper

3B bonded pencil on tracing paper
Left: 2B bonded pencil—6B woodless—Strathmore kid finish with gesso coating

These illustrations represent a change of pace from the one on the preceding page. Instead of a deliberate and controlled handling of the pencil, the artist has used a searching, sketchy, continuously moving line.

Any subject is fine for this approach. Have a lot of sharpened pencils handy and don't worry about erasing. Begin at whatever point attracts your eye. Treat your pencil as if it were an explorer. Let it go back and forth and around the object you are drawing. If you want tone, turn your pencil on its side (woodless pencils are particularly good for this).

When do you stop? How do you keep the drawing from being overworked? That is the hardest question for an artist to answer. There is no rule that you can apply—just your own instinct that you have done enough to make the drawing have "life." How do you develop that instinct? By doing many drawings. From experience you'll learn when enough is enough.

These two pictures illustrate two variations on another approach to pencil drawing: crosshatching—using lines to create tones and patterns.

On this page the tones are developed through line only; the darkest areas occur where there is the greatest amount of crosshatching. This approach tends to produce a more stylized or patterned drawing. The drawing on the facing page, however, is a more naturalistic study of a tree. Here, the lines and crosshatching were done over a base of shading which gives definition and dark accents to the drawing.

H-2B on somerset satin (smooth finish) paper,
graphite stick for base tones, B-6B for line work, somerset paper with textured finish

B-5B, saunders paper

Here are two more drawings that use patterns. On this page lines are used to suggest the patterns that exist in nature; notice the contrast between the thorny pattern of the foreground tree and the soft, rounded trees in the background. Contrast is also the theme of the drawing on the facing page. Detailed linear patterns on the wall set off the various tones on the woman and the cushion. The use of a graphite stick for her shirt suggests both its pattern and texture. The soft tones of the hair give greater weight to the simple line drawing of the face and hands.

When you do this type of study, remember to be selective. Don't try to reproduce every detail of every pattern. Remember, as an illustrator, you determine what your audience sees. Only show what is important to the story behind the picture.

B-5B and graphite stick, saunders paper

HB-B on vellum tracing paper

24

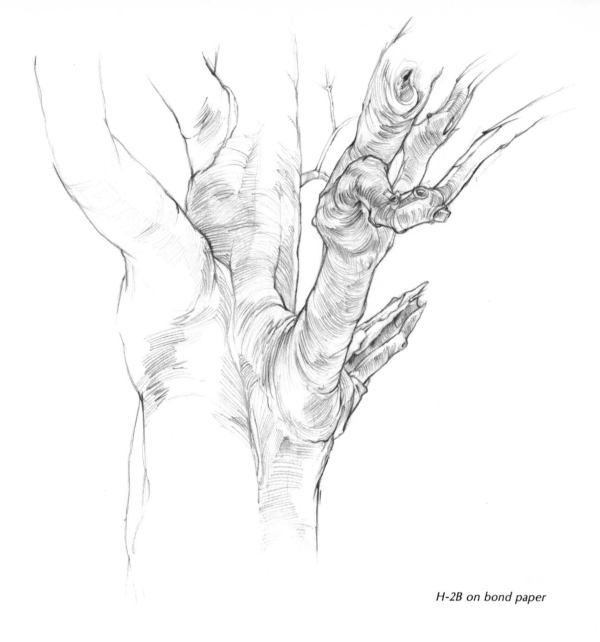

H-2B on bond paper

These pages show two drawings from nature. These studies develop your ability to really see what an object is. Use pointed pencils (nothing darker than a 2B) and paper that takes a certain amount of erasing. Make sure you are comfortable and prepare to spend at least two to three hours (maybe more) doing the drawing. Use only line and leave out all unnecessary background material. Concentrate on the organic structure of the plant or tree. When you look at your drawings later, you should be able to sense the weight and solidity of the tree and the delicacy of the flower.

Both drawings: 3B on vellum tracing paper

These pictures are also drawn from life, but they are very different kinds of drawings. They record the decorative aspects of the world around us. Buildings and other man-made structures are ideal subjects for this kind of drawing.

Set yourself up in front of a store, a vegetable stand, or some other interesting scene with lots of decorative detail and eye appeal. Use a sharpened soft pencil; select a large sheet of paper with enough room for your pencil to wander. Start at one corner and continue to draw until you fill the space.

Your eye will select or reject various details as your pencil moves over the page. Don't sketch lines in first or go over lines. Try drawing without taking your eyes off the subject. After you've finished, you can go back and add or remove a detail or two. But don't fuss over the lines. They should look fresh.

4B graphite stick, 2B-5B bonded pencil, 6B woodless pencil on tracing paper, kneaded eraser highlights

C H A P T E R 3

Structure

We have seen how drawing different subjects can be helpful, both to the development of your pencil technique and your skill as an illustrator. Now we come to another approach to drawing, one which at first might seem less personal. Let's call it the world of shapes, of three-dimensional forms or volumes. These cylinders, cones, boxes, and spheres are, in one way or another, the basis of all the forms around us.

The study of these forms offers opportunities to explore the tonal and shading potential of the pencil. The drawings that result will then become the basis for illustrations of barns, houses, silos, cars, and other familiar structures.

Some of these forms, whether manufactured or natural, might seem at first very difficult and complicated to draw. A landscape, for example, with mountains and trees, is so vast that it is hard to know where and how to begin. Ancient Chinese landscape artists had the same problem. Their solution was to study and draw the miniature gardens and landscapes that were in their own courtyards. In this way, they could make studies of rock and plant forms at close range. They could also move around the subjects and draw them from many points of view. This basic technique is still used today by artists and architects to get a better understanding of the three-dimensional world.

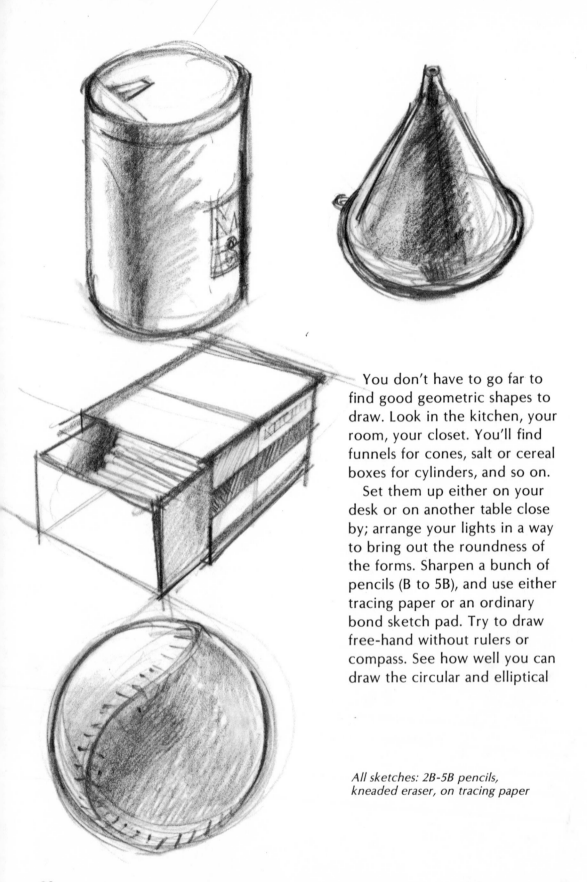

You don't have to go far to find good geometric shapes to draw. Look in the kitchen, your room, your closet. You'll find funnels for cones, salt or cereal boxes for cylinders, and so on.

Set them up either on your desk or on another table close by; arrange your lights in a way to bring out the roundness of the forms. Sharpen a bunch of pencils (B to 5B), and use either tracing paper or an ordinary bond sketch pad. Try to draw free-hand without rulers or compass. See how well you can draw the circular and elliptical

All sketches: 2B-5B pencils, kneaded eraser, on tracing paper

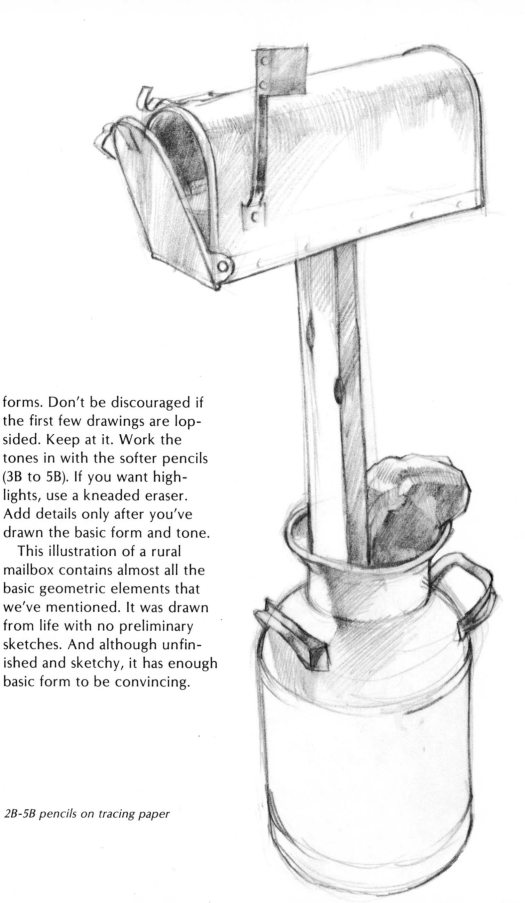

forms. Don't be discouraged if the first few drawings are lop-sided. Keep at it. Work the tones in with the softer pencils (3B to 5B). If you want high-lights, use a kneaded eraser. Add details only after you've drawn the basic form and tone.

This illustration of a rural mailbox contains almost all the basic geometric elements that we've mentioned. It was drawn from life with no preliminary sketches. And although unfin-ished and sketchy, it has enough basic form to be convincing.

2B-5B pencils on tracing paper

There is a big difference in size between a cereal box and a farm silo. But both are cylinders. An illustrator can apply the principles of drawing and shading of one of these objects to the other.

This sequence of pictures demonstrates how the lessons learned drawing simple objects at your desk can be applied to drawings of a larger scale. The first step is the selection of your point of view. The interest here is the contrast between the tall silo and the low barn.

Next, lightly sketch (with the pencil point) the various forms. When you are satisfied with the composition, put in some broad tonal areas, either with a graphite stick or the side of a woodless pencil. Finally, use your dark pencils and kneaded eraser to add dark and light accents.

All drawings: Graphite stick and 2B pencil on visualizing paper

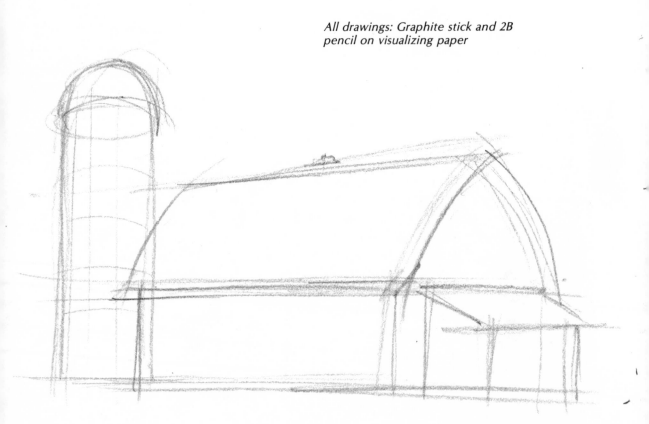

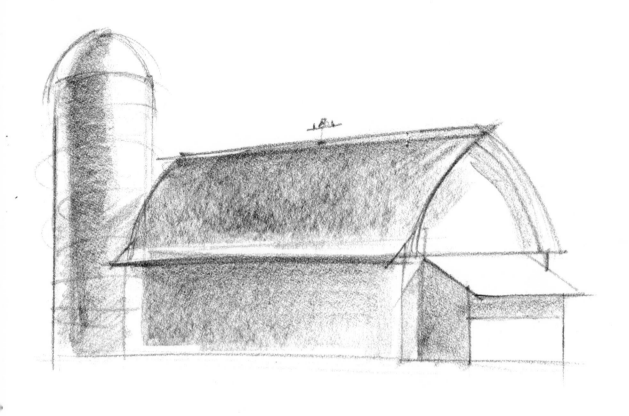

Graphite stick, 2B-6B woodless pencils on gesso covered paper.

Both sketches: 2B-6B woodless pencils, graphite stick, visualizing paper.

Illustrators often are required to portray complex scenes; rooms with doors that lead into other rooms with open windows, for example. This scene offers that kind of challenge. The objective here is to portray the barn complex from close up rather than from a distance (as on pages 32-33).

Using the same tools, a graphite stick and soft pencil, the artist roughed in several compositions (two are presented here). These are done quickly, but notice that the basic forms and shaded areas are clearly defined. The artist finally decided to get closer to one of the barns for the final illustration.

To achieve the effect of old barn wood, the artist used a gesso ground. The texture was created by rubbing a graphite stick over the gesso.

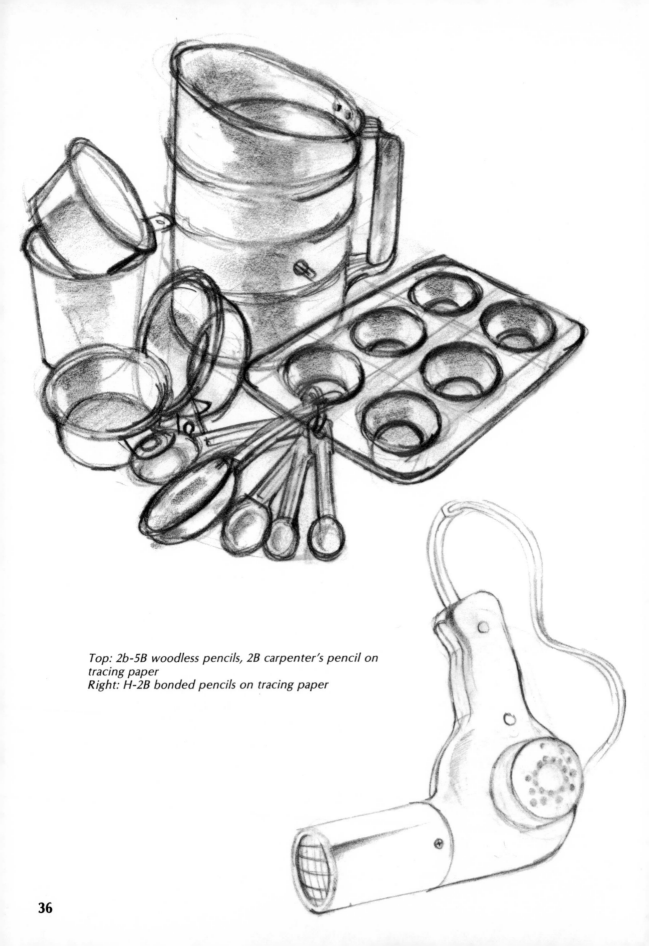

Top: 2b-5B woodless pencils, 2B carpenter's pencil on tracing paper
Right: H-2B bonded pencils on tracing paper

HB-3B bonded and woodless pencils on visualizing paper

Here are three more examples of how the tonal properties of pencil can be used to explore the structure of an object. The baking utensils are variations on a curved surface. This is a good opportunity to study highlights on metal. This is a preliminary drawing, done from the objects. This drawing could then be put on a lightbox to be the guide for a more carefully rendered drawing. That is what was done for the hair dryer. This illustration was traced from a previous rough sketch. Here the artist used subtle shading to suggest the white plastic surface.

The Land Rover was sketched from life. Here again, we see very basic shapes and surfaces. Although this could be a preliminary sketch for a more finished drawing, it could also stand on its own as an illustration for an adventure story set in Africa or some other setting with rugged terrain.

Most of the studies of form and structure we have covered in this chapter emphasized various shading techniques. A different pencil technique for exploring structure is illustrated by these two drawings. This technique (see page 25) requires very careful study of the object. It is almost totally linear in approach; even tonal areas are achieved by close grouping of lines. The main objective of this kind of study is to develop an understanding of volume. For example, when drawing the front of the doll's knee, imagine your pencil going completely around to the back of the knee. This will help you to be aware that everything—a knee, a ball, a glove—has three dimensions.

When you first do this type of drawing, pick something you are familiar with; something you know very well. In your drawing of that object try to imagine that you are picking it up and feeling its weight.

Both drawings: H-2B bonded pencils on vellum tracing paper

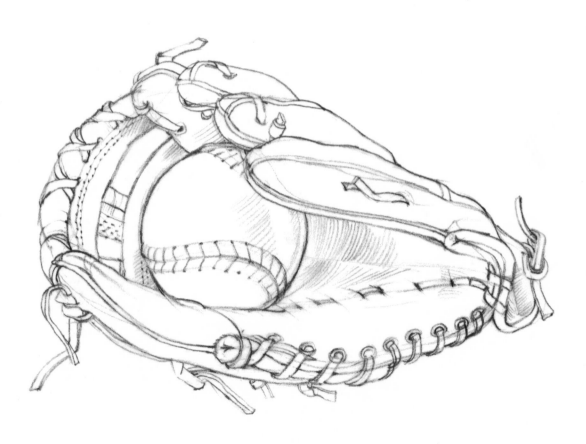

2H mechanical pencil, HB-2B bonded pencil, kneaded eraser on Head 100% rag paper

40

C H A P T E R 4

Style

Style is a word that is often used in discussing art. Most successful illustrators are especially noted for their individual styles. And, of course, every young artist is eager to develop a recognizable style. But what is style, and how does an artist "get" it?

For one thing, a personal style is the result of experience; it does not appear overnight. The more you practice your pencil drawing, the more personal your technique will become. But a drawing style is more than good pencil technique. It is also an expression of yourself. It is not like a coat that you put on and take off. It is more like the expression on your face or the way you walk or laugh. It is part of you.

Style also reflects your interests, the subjects you like to draw, and what you feel about them. Famous artists and illustrators are often remembered by the subject matter they have used in their work.

This kind of attachment is important in the development of style, and a student of illustration can encourage its growth. The process is really very natural, and it's probably already happening. How do you know? Just ask yourself these questions: What do I like to draw? Why do I prefer a pencil to other tools? How do I like to draw? How do I draw my favorite subjects, from up close or far away? Do I concentrate on details or am I more interested in light and shadow? The answers to such questions will help you to become more sensitive to the work you've done and are doing.

These three illustrations are examples of a worthwhile experiment. Pick a subject that interests you. Draw it using at least three different pencil techniques: a strictly linear approach, combined line and tone, and only tones. Use different papers: smooth for line, lightly textured for the combination, and very textured for the tonal drawing.

You will discover that each of these approaches will reveal something about the subject. The linear, with its attention to detail, will bring out the decorative aspects; the line-and-tone will emphasize the subject's form; and the rough-textured tonal rendering will suggest moods of drama and mystery.

When you've done some of these studies and variations, look at them and ask yourself which direction or effect interests you most.

Far Left: H-HB bonded pencils on strathmore kid finish
Left: H-3B bonded pencils on whatman paper
Right: Charcoal and carbon pencils, chinese white pencil, eraser, finger smudge on watercolor paper

2B on tracing paper

If you were to start with only the basic figure drawing (above), how would you develop it? It is clear from the solution that the decorative aspect is the real interest of this illustrator.

Using the basic drawing as a guide, try some of your own variations. This is also a good opportunity for you to begin learning

H-3B on tracing paper

about research. How to find good source material for pictures is something every illustrator must learn. Look for a book that uses pencil to illustrate costumes. You will find it helpful and stimulating to your imagination—and you will also see how other artists have used pencil to render detail.

There is a wealth of source material close to home—even in your own room. Illustrators frequently use their own surroundings and family as subjects. You might begin by drawing what is on your desk, just as you find it. Or you might draw the freshly laundered shirt that is hanging on your closet door.

In these two pictures there seems to be a relationship between the shirt and the objects on the desk: they are both drawings that tell something about the person who drew them. They are a little like self-portraits without the actual person—portraits of a personality.

Both drawings: 2H-3B bonded pencils on whatman paper

A drawing of a sketchbook. Bound notebooks make it easier for you to keep a record of your progress.

As you continue to explore your own world, use a bound notebook to record your sketches and impressions. Bring it with you to school, the park, wherever your interests take you. Have it handy, with some sharpened pencils, when you are with your family, friends, and pets. You will find that these notebooks will be a valuable source of ideas and research material.

All sketches: 2B bonded pencils on notebook (visualizing) paper

49

When you have gained some confidence in your drawing ability and feel more comfortable with the pencil, try doing some
portraits. You (and your models) might find it more fun if costumes or some form of outlandish or over-sized clothing is used
in the pose. You might even put on a costume yourself and try a
self-portrait.

The pictures in this chapter are only suggestions. It is up to
you to discover what subjects really interest you and which of
the pencil techniques you are most comfortable with.

As you do more drawings, you will begin to understand what
you enjoy most about working in pencil. With enjoyment, understanding, and practice, your talent will develop along a path
that will eventually lead to a style of your own.

All drawings: B-3B bonded and woodless pencils on visualizing paper

3B bonded pencil on notebook (tracing) paper

C H A P T E R 5

Sketch to Finish

It is always interesting to leaf through an illustrator's sketchbook. Looking at all the pencil drawings—some of them sketches from life, others from the imagination—is like looking through a peep-hole into the artist's mind. You begin to understand how picture ideas are born. But how does an illustrator transform simple pencil drawings from a sketchbook into finished pencil illustrations that will be printed in books and magazines?

To begin with, an artist's sketchbook is a catch-all. Whatever catches the artist's eye goes in. Sometimes these sketches are done with a specific purpose in mind. More often, the drawings and doodles simply reflect the things that arouse the artist's curiosity. Later, when the illustrator is asked to do a specific drawing, the sketchbooks become a reference source. If some of the material in them is appropriate, it will be incorporated into the artist's compositional sketches. In these, the artist tries to capture the mood and meaning of the story behind the illustration.

The illustration that concludes this chapter (on page 63) was created exactly like that. The story the artist was asked to illustrate included a clown and his dog. The clown in the story is faced with a decision that concerns his career, and the pictures must express that.

In one of the artist's sketchbooks was a series of pencil drawings done during a visit to the circus. There were also many drawings of the family dog and random studies of people. From these, the artist selected several sketches that seemed appropriate for this assignment.

All drawings traced from notebook on vellum tracing, B-5B bonded pencils

All sketches: 2B-5B woodless pencils on tracing paper

However, the illustrator first had to decide on the composition of the picture. A series of small, "thumbnail" sketches were done, primarily for composition. Thumbnail sketches answer such questions as: Should the entire figure be included? Should the figure be sitting, standing, or lying down? Should the figure of the clown be in the foreground? Should only the face be used? In the beginning, the artist had many options. These small sketches narrowed down the choices. The sketches also served as tests for light and dark elements.

*Both drawings: H-3B
bonded pencils on tracing
paper*

When the composition had been decided upon, the artist
looked at the notebook sketches that had been set aside. Two of
them were perfect for the new picture, except that one drawing
was of a man in ordinary street clothes, not a clown's costume.

Working with tracing paper and a lightbox, the illustrator was
able to combine two of the sketches into one composition. At
the same time, the illustrator was also able to transform the sitting man into a clown by changing details of the man's clothing.

A top view of a lightbox. There are three separate drawings on tracing paper: a) drawing of dog; b) drawing of seated man; c) large sheet with drawing of clown and—when finished—the dog. Tape (d) is used to hold sheets on to the lightbox.

Detail and tone were added to the picture as more and more
sketches were made. (Each new sketch used the basic composition, page 59, as a guide.) In these sketches the illustrator was
seeking to capture something special.

Both drawings: 2B and 3B bonded pencils on tracing paper

   The artist felt that the sketches weren't quite right. The seated pose of the clown and dog was too static. The picture needed more life and movement, something that would be more expressive of the circus.

Both sketches: 4B woodless pencil on tracing paper

At first the artist thought the drawing at top left was the answer. But the dog's head appearing over the clown's shoulder produced a disturbing design; it was difficult for the viewer to understand what was happening. The artist made an important decision. To get a more effective illustration, the dog was eliminated.

Now the clown is the only focus of interest. His eyes are glued to the spinning ball as he tries to balance it. The lights of the big top cast dramatic shadows on his costume and face. And the broadly painted clown smile does not completely hide the sadness in his face.

This is the impression the illustrator was trying to achieve. And in order to accomplish that, several changes—even fresh starts—had to be made.

Don't be discouraged if your drawings are not always up to your expectations. Try again and again. The satisfaction that comes from drawing is worth the effort.

HB-3B bonded pencils, 4B-6B woodless pencils, kneaded eraser for highlights on saunders paper

Index